Jesus Visits the Nephites

written by Tiffany Thomas
illustrated by Nikki Casassa

CFI · An imprint of Cedar Fort, Inc. · Springville, Utah

HARD WORDS:
forget, earth shakes

PARENT TIP: There are many double letters in this story: pretty, marry, all. Point out that your child does not have to say the letter two times.

This is Nephi.
He is a man of God.

Nephi tells the people Jesus will be born.

3

Jesus is born
and there is a
new star.
The Nephites
see the sun
for three days.

4

A long time goes by.
Many Nephites forget
they saw the new star.

The bad Nephites want to get rid of the good Nephites.

Nephi prays.
God says
Jesus will die.

Jesus dies.

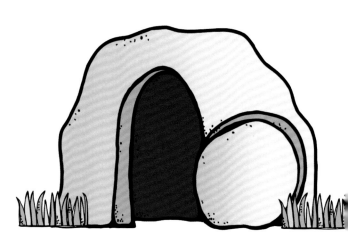

There are a lot of fires
and the earth shakes.

It is dark for three days.

The sun comes back.

Jesus comes
down from
the sky.

The end.

This is not an official publication of The Church of Jesus Christ of Latter-day Saints. The opinions and views expressed herein belong solely to the author and do not necessarily represent the opinions or views of Cedar Fort, Inc. Permission for the use of sources, graphics, and photos is also solely the responsibility of the author.

ISBN 13: 978-1-4621-4337-5

Published by CFI, an imprint of Cedar Fort, Inc. • 2373 W. 700 S., Suite 100, Springville, UT 84663
Distributed by Cedar Fort, Inc., www.cedarfort.com

Cover design and interior layout design by Shawnda T. Craig
Cover design © 2022 Cedar Fort, Inc.
Printed in China • Printed on acid-free paper
10 9 8 7 6 5 4 3 2 1